Spot the Difference

Legs

Diyan Leake

Heinemann Library
Chicago, Illinois

Customer Service 888-454-2279
Visit our website at www.heinemannraintree.com

Designed by Joanna Hinton-Malivoire
Printed in China by South China Printing Company Limited

12 11 10 09 08
10 9 8 7 6 5 4 3 2 1

ISBN-10: 1-4329-0001-3 (hc)
ISBN-10: 1-4329-0006-4 (pb)

The Library of Congress has cataloged the first edition as follows:
Leake, Diyan.
  Legs / Diyan Leake. -- 1st ed.
      p. cm. -- (Spot the difference)
  Includes bibliographical references and index.
  ISBN 978-1-4329-0001-4 (hc) -- ISBN 978-1-4329-0006-9 (pb)
  1. Leg--Juvenile literature. I. Title.
  QL950.7.L44 2007
  573.9'98331--dc22
                                    2007010529

Acknowledgments
The author and publisher are grateful to the following for permission to reproduce photographs: Alamy/Juniors Bildarchiv p. **17**; Alamy/Visual&Written SL pp. **16**, **23** top; Corbis pp. **7**, **9**, **back cover**; Corbis/LWA-Dann Tardif p. **20**; Nature Picture Library pp. **4** (Sue Flood), **8** (Tony Heald), **12** (Anup Shah), **13** (Staffan Widstrand), **14** (Kim Taylor), **18** (Doug Wechsler), **22** (Doug Wechsler); Photolibrary pp. **5** (Mike Powles), **15** (Philippe Bonduel); Photolibrary/Animals Animals/Earth Scenes pp. **10**, **19**, **22**; Photolibrary/Mauritius Die Bildagentur Gmbh p. **21**; Photolibrary/Picture Press p. **11**; Punchstock/Digital Archive Japan p. **6**.

Cover photograph of an Arizona mantid reproduced with permission of Alamy (Bob Jensen).

Contents

What Are Legs? 4

Why Do Animals Have Legs? 6

Different Legs 8

Amazing Legs 14

Your Legs 20

Spot the Difference! 22

Picture Glossary 23

Index 24

What Are Legs?

Many animals have legs.

Many animals use their legs to move.

Why Do Animals Have Legs?

Animals use their legs to stand.

Animals use their legs to run.

Different Legs

Legs come in many shapes.
Legs come in many sizes.

This is a giraffe.
It has four long legs.

This is a heron.
It has two long legs.

This is a wren.
It has two short legs.

This is a rhinoceros.
It has thick legs.

This is a kangaroo.
It has thin legs.

Amazing Legs

This is a bug.

It can walk on water.

ear

This is a cricket.
It can hear with its legs.

This is a flamingo.
Its legs bend backwards.

This is a horse.
Its legs bend, too.

This is a spider.
It has eight legs.

This is a millipede.
It has lots of legs.

Your Legs

People have legs, too.

People use their legs to move.

People are like other animals.

Spot the Difference!

Which animal has eight legs?

Which animal has lots of legs?

Picture Glossary

 **flamingo** large pink bird with long legs

 **heron** large bird with long legs, a long neck, and a long, sharp beak

 **wren** tiny bird with brown feathers

Index

bug, 14

cricket, 15

flamingo, 16, 23

giraffe, 9

heron, 10, 23

horse, 17

kangaroo, 13

millipede, 19, 22

people, 20, 21

rhinoceros, 12

spider, 18, 22

wren, 11, 23

Note to Parents and Teachers

Before reading

Talk to the children about animals' legs. What can animals do with their legs? Can the children think of animals with two legs? Four legs? Six legs? Eight legs? Talk about kangaroos which have four legs but only use two legs to move.

After reading

- Make a chart with four columns. Write the heading: How many legs? Then head the columns 2, 4, 6, 8. Invite children to draw small pictures of animals or cut out pictures. Tell them to stick their picture in the correct column.
- Tell the children they are going to move like different animals. For example, tell them to waddle like a duck, hop like a rabbit, jump like a kangaroo, or run like a cheetah.
- Stand the children in a circle. Say the rhyme and complete the actions: "With my legs I run, run, run. With my legs I jump, jump, jump. Run and jump. Run and jump. All around the circle." Repeat with "hop" and "skip."